Introduction

In this book, you will see 30 recipes with an ingredient (garlic)

Basically this ingredient will be used as a flavor addition

The book is intended for daily cooking

Healthy Chicken Pot Pie

YIELD: **4 SUBMITTINGS**
PREP TIME:
TEN MINS
COOK TIME:
45 MINS
TOTAL TIME:
1 HR

Ingredients

- one tbsp extra-virgin olive oil
- ten ounces cremini baby bella mushrooms
- one cup diced carrots — *approximately 3 average*
- half cup diced celery — *approximately one big stalk*
- one half tsps garlic powder
- half tsp kosher salt
- One-quarter tsp black pepper
- One-quarter cup all-purpose flour
- two cups unsweetened almond milk
- two cups prepared and shredded boneless, skinless chicken breasts* — *approximately 8 ounces either two small breasts*
- half cup chilled peas
- half cup chilled pearl onions
- one tbsp sliced fresh thyme
- one prepared pie peel — *dairy free supposing needed (I used my loved whole wwarmth pie peel)*
- one egg — *slightly beaten with one tbsp water to Make some egg wash*

Instructions

1. Prewarmth the oven to 425 degrees F. slightly coat a 9-inch pie dish with baking spray. put aside.

2. Warmth a big Dutch oven either similar deep, heavy-downed pan over average-high heat. place the oil to the pan. As hot, place the mushrooms and prepare for 8 mins, till mushrooms are beginning to brown, mixing sometimes. place the carrots, celery, garlic powder, salt, and pepper. prepare till the mushrooms have browned more deeply and the carrots begin to soften, approximately 3 additional mins.

3. Strew the flour over the top of the vegetables and prepare two mins. Slowly pour within the almondmilk, adding a several splashes at a time, mixing constantly. Bring to a poor boil, scraping any brown bits from the down of the pan. Keep to allow bubble till thickened, approximately 3 to 5 mins. Stir within the chicken, peas, onions, and thyme. Spoon the chicken mix in the prepared pie dish.

4. Roll the pie dough in a circle big enough to overlay your dish. Brush the edges of the pie dish with the egg wash, then place the dough over the top so that this overhangs the edges. Trim the overhang to a half inch bigr than edge of the dish. Carefully Put the dough onto the edges of the dish so that this sticks, then brush all over with the remaining egg wash. With a sharp knife, slice 3 slits within the top.

5. Bake till hot and bubbly on the inside and the peel is deeply golden, approximately 25 mins. allow rest a several mins. submit hot.

Recipe Notes

- The filling possibly prepared ahead of time and stored within the refrigerator for 3 days either chilled for up to 3 months (let thaw overnight within the refrigerator). place the peel simply before baking.

- This recipe tastes best the day this is made because the peel is the most crisp, however you'll keep leftovers within the refrigerator for up to 4 days. Rewarmth carefully within the microwave either oven.

- To prepare the recipe vegetarian, substitute some additional two cups of sliced vegetables for the chicken. The pot pie can still be delicious and hearty.

- To prepare gluten free, employyour loved gluten free pie peel.

- The calorie count was updated on 3/5/19 from 335 calories to 380 calories to reflect new nutritional data. That said, this is meant to be some estimate and provided as a courtesy, so supposing you'd like more precise measurements, I advised calculating this on your own employing your online calorie calculator of choice.

Roasted <u>Broccoli</u> and Carrots

YIELD: **4 SUBMITTINGS**
PREP TIME:
15 MINS
COOK TIME:
20 MINS
TOTAL TIME:
35 MINS

Ingredients

- 6 average carrots — *peeled (approximately ten ounces)*
- one big head <u>broccoli</u> — *slice in florets (approximately 3 cups florets)*
- one half tsps Italian seasoning
- half tsp kosher salt
- half tsp garlic powder
- half tsp onion powder
- One-quarter tsp black pepper
- two tbsp extra-virgin olive oil
- 3 tbsp delicately grated Parmesan cheese — *if you want for submitting*

Instructions

1. Prewarmth the oven to 400 degrees F. Generously coat a big rimmed <u>baking</u> sheet with non-stick spray.

2. Supposing the carrots are thick, slice them in half lengthwise. Slice diagonally in one ½-inch thick slices, then place the carrots within the middle of the <u>baking</u> sheet. place the <u>broccoli</u> florets to the <u>baking</u> sheet with the carrots.

3. In a small bowl, stir along the Italian seasoning, salt, pepper, garlic powder, and onion powder. Drizzle the <u>vegetables</u> with the oil, then strew on the spice mix. Toss to coat the <u>vegetables</u> evenly, then unfold them in some even layer.

4. Place within the oven and roast for 20 mins, till they are browned and tender, tossing as halfway through. Strew with Parmesan. Enjoy hot.

Recipe Notes

- **TO STORE**: Place leftovers in some airtight storage container within the refrigerator for up to 4 days.
- **TO REHEAT**: Rewarm <u>broccoli</u> and carrots on a <u>baking</u> sheet within the oven at 350 degrees F till hot. You'll also rewarmth the <u>vegetables</u> within the microwave.
- **TO FREEZE**: Keep the <u>vegetables</u> in some airtight freezer-safe storage container within the freezer for up to 3 months. allow thaw overnight within the refrigerator before reheating.

Zucchini *Stir Fry*

YIELD: **4 SUBMITTINGS**
PREP TIME:
TEN MINS
COOK TIME:
15 MINS
TOTAL TIME:
25 MINS

Ingredients

- one pound boneless — *skinless chicken breasts (or thighs either tenders), thinly sliced then slice in bite-sized pieces*
- 4 tbsp poor sodium soy gravy — *divided*
- two tsps apple cider vinegar — *divided*
- two tsps granulated sugar — *divided*
- one tbsp minced fresh ginger
- 3 cloves minced garlic — *approximately one tbsp*
- two tbsp water
- one tsp cornstarch
- One-quarter tsp red pepper flakes
- two average zucchini — *yellow squash, either a mix*
- one big red either yellow onion
- two tbsp extra virgin olive oil
- Sesame seeds — *if you want for garnish*
- Sliced green onion — *for garnish*

Instructions

1. In a big bowl, mix the chicken, one tbsp soy sauce, one tsp apple cider vinegar, and one tsp granulated sugar. put aside whereas you prep the remaining ingredients.

2. In a small bowl either big liquid measuring cup, stir along the remaining 3 tbsp soy sauce, remaining one tsp apple cider vinegar, remaining one tsp sugar, the ginger, garlic, water, cornstarch, and red pepper flakes. put aside.

3. Trim off the ends of the zucchini. Slice in half lengthwise, then place the flat, slice sides on the counter. Chop crosswise in ¼-inch thick half moons. Thinly chop the onion.

4. In a wide skillet, warmth one tbsp of the olive oil over average-high heat. As the oil is hot, place the chicken and its marinating liquid. Fry till the chicken is golden brown on the outsides and fully prepared through, approximately 3 to 4 mins. Take away to a plate.

5. Warmth the remaining one tbsp oil. place the onion. prepare till tender and beginning to brown, 4 to 5 mins.

6. Give the gravy one more stir, then place this to the pan. allow prepare 30 seconds, then place the sliced <u>zucchini</u>. prepare simply till the <u>zucchini</u> begins to soften, approximately 3 mins more.

7. Take away from the heat, then stir within the reserved chicken. submit hot with a strew of sesame seeds and green onion as desired.

Recipe Notes

- **TO STORE**: Leftovers possibly stored in some airtight storage container within the refrigerator for up to 4 days.
- **TO REHEAT**: Carefully rewarm <u>zucchini</u> stir fry in a big skillet on the stovetop over average-low heat. You'll also rewarmth this dish within the microwave.
- **TO FREEZE**: Place leftovers in some airtight freezer-safe storage container within the freezer for up to 3 months. allow thaw overnight within the refrigerator before reheating.

Cucumber Tomato Avocado Salad

YIELD: **6 SUBMITTINGS**
PREP TIME:
20 MINS
TOTAL TIME:
20 MINS

Ingredients

FOR THE CUCUMBER TOMATO AVOCADO SALAD:

- ½ small red onion — *thinly sliced*
- one big English cucumber — *quartered lengthwise and sliced*
- one pint halved cherry tomatoes — *approximately two cups*
- two average avocados — *peeled, pitted, and diced*
- one-third cup crumbled feta cheese — *divided*
- One-quarter cup sliced fresh cilantro (or dill)

FOR THE DRESSING:

- 3 tbsp fresh lime juice — *from approximately two small limes*
- one tbsp extra-virgin olive oil
- two tsps honey
- two cloves minced garlic (approximately one tsp)
- half tsp kosher salt
- half tsp black pepper

Instructions

1. Place the sliced red onions in a small bowl and overlay them with cold water (this helps take away some of the onions' harsh bite).

2. In a small bowl either big measuring cup, blend along the dressing ingredients: Lime juice, olive oil, honey, garlic, salt, and pepper.

3. In a very big bowl, place the cucumbers, tomatoes, avocado, half of the feta, and cilantro. Drain the red onion, then place this to the bowl. Pour the dressing over the top, then stir very carefully to mix. Strew the remaining feta over the top. Enjoy instantly either overlay the bowl with plastic cover and refrigerate for up to 4 hours. Give the mix a gentle stir simply before submitting.

Recipe Notes

- Keep leftovers within the refrigerator for up to one day. The avocado can brown slightly and the vegetables can become more liquidy, however the salad can still taste delicious.

Vegan **Stuffed Peppers**

YIELD: **8 PEPPER HALVES (4 TO 6 SUBMITTINGS)**
PREP TIME:
5 MINS
COOK TIME:
1 HR 5 MINS
TOTAL TIME:
1 HR TEN MINS

Ingredients

- two tbsp extra virgin olive oil — *divided*
- one small yellow onion — *sliced*
- ½ cup lentils — *I like French green lentils (lentils du puy, which hold their shape; brown lentils can also work. red either yellow lentils are less adviseded as they can become mushy)*
- half cup unprepared quinoa
- two tsps Italian seasoning
- half tsp kosher salt — *plus additional for <u>baking</u> the peppers*
- ¼ tsp red pepper flakes — *either up to ½ tsp supposing you like more spicy*
- two cloves garlic — *minced (approximately two tsps)*
- one cup poor sodium <u>vegetable</u> bouillon — *plus additional as needed*
- one 15-ounce can fire-roasted diced <u>tomato</u>es within their juices
- half cup sliced sun-dried <u>tomato</u>es — *dried packed and rehydrated either packed in oil, drained and patted dry**
- 3 tbsp nutritional yeast — *either Parmesan supposing you Dont must the peppers <u>vegan</u>*
- 4 big red bell peppers
- If you want: ¼ to ½ cup non-dairy mozzarella "cheese" either cashew <u>cream</u>
- two tbsp sliced fresh basil, parsley, either a mix

Instructions

1. Warmth one tbsp of the oil in a Dutch oven either similar big, sturdy-downed pot over average heat. place the onion and prepare for 5 mins, either till the onion is beginning to soften, mixing sometimes. place the Italian seasoning, ½ tsp kosher salt, red pepper flakes, and garlic. allow prepare simply till the garlic is fragrant, approximately 30 seconds.
2. Add the lentils, quinoa, broth, fire-roasted <u>tomato</u>es, and sun-dried <u>tomato</u>es. Bring the mix to a boil, then decrease warmth to low. Overlay and simmer for 25 to 28 mins, either till the lentils are tender. Stir as halfway through, then again towards the end of the cooking time. Supposing the mix looks too dry, splash in additional bouillon either water. Stir within the nutritional yeast.
3. Whereas the lentils and quinoa cook, prewarmth your oven to 400 degrees F. slightly coat a 9x13-inch <u>baking</u> dish with nonstick spray. Chop the bell peppers in half from top to down (I slice right down through the stems). Take away the seeds and membranes then place slice side up within the prepared <u>baking</u> dish. Drizzle the insides with the remaining one tbsp oil and strew slightly with salt. Attentively pour a thin stratum of water in the down of the pan. Place within the oven and bake, uncovered, for 20 mins. This step gives the peppers a head start whereas the filling finishes up.

4. Attentively mound the prepared filling inside of the peppers. Supposing employing a non-dairy "mozzarella" strew this on top. Comeback the pan to the oven and Prepare in oven for 5 to ten additional mins, till the peppers are completely tender and the filling is piping hot. Strew with fresh basil and enjoy!

Recipe Notes

- **TO STORE**: Keep leftover stuffed peppers in some airtight storage container within the refrigerator for up to 4 days.
- **TO REHEAT**: Rewarmth carefully within the microwave either oven at 350 degrees F. Slice the peppers in a several pieces before reheating so that they warm evenly.
- **TO FREEZE**: Chill leftover peppers in some airtight freezer-safe storage container for up to 3 months. allow thaw overnight within the refrigerator before reheating.

*Supposing your sun-dried tomatoes are dried packed, rehydrate them before starting the recipe. Chop them, and place them in a covered bowl of hot water. When approximately 5 mins, drain the water and pat the tomatoes dry. employin the recipe as directed.

Zucchini *Fries*

YIELD: **6 SUBMITTINGS (APPROXIMATELY 48 FRIES)**
PREP TIME:
20 MINS
COOK TIME:
20 MINS
TOTAL TIME:
40 MINS

Ingredients

FOR THE ZUCCHINI FRIES:

- 3 average 7-inch zucchini — *slice in half inch x 3 half-inch "sticks" (approximately one One-quarter pounds)*
- half cup Panko breadcrumbs
- one-third cup white whole wwarmth flour — *either all-purpose flour*
- One-quarter cup delicately grated Parmesan cheese
- half tsp kosher salt
- ¼ tsp onion powder
- One-quarter tsp ground black pepper
- two big egg whites
- Nonstick cooking spatter — *olive oil either canola oil flavored*

FOR THE BASIL DIPPING SAUCE:

- half cup non-fat plain Greek yogurt
- two tbsp sliced fresh basil — *either ½ tsp dried basil*
- one clove minced garlic — *approximately one tsp*
- ¼ tsp Worcestershire sauce
- 1/8 tsp kosher salt
- 1/8 ground black pepper

Instructions

1. Make the fries: Position racks within the middle of your oven and prewarmth the oven to 425 degrees F. Coat a big, rimmed baking sheet with nonstick spray.

2. Spread the sliced zucchini onto paper towels either a damp kitchen towel. slightly pat dry. allow rest on the towels whereas you prepare the coating.

3. In wide, shallow dish (a pie dish works good) mix the Panko, flour, Parmesan, salt, onion powder, and pepper. In a else bowl that is big enough to coat the zucchini, briskly blend the egg whites till slightly foamy.

4. Operating five either six zucchini fries at a time, place the zucchini within the bowl with the egg whites, tossing to coat them evenly. Shake off any glut egg white, then place them to the bowl with the Panko. Coat them with the Panko, Puting this on slightly so that this adheres. place the zucchini on the baking sheet. Line up the sticks so that they are near every else and all fit, however prepare sure they Dont touch. recur with remaining zucchini.

5. Lightly however thoroughly coat the exposed sides of the zucchini with the cooking spray. Prepare in oven for ten mins, then take away from the oven and slightly coat with baking spatter as more. Comeback to the oven, rotating the pan 180 degrees, then

keep <u>baking</u> for ten additional mins, till the crumbles are crisp and golden and the insides are tender.

6. Whereas the <u>zucchini</u> bakes, prepare the dipping sauce. In a small mixing bowl, blend along all of the ingredients: the <u>Greek yogurt</u>, basil, garlic, Worcestershire, salt, and paper. Taste and adsimply the seasoning as desired. submit the fries immediately, with the gravy for dipping.

Recipe Notes

- **TO STORE**: Place leftover <u>zucchini</u> fries in some airtight storage container within the refrigerator for up to two days.
- **TO REHEAT**: For best results, rewarm the <u>zucchini</u> fries within the oven at 375 degrees F on a <u>baking</u> sheet coated with nonstick spray. Dont rewarmth fries within the microwave—the possibly come mushy.

Instant Pot Chicken and *Rice*

YIELD: **6 SUBMITTINGS, APPROXIMATELY TEN CUPS**
PREP TIME:
15 MINS
COOK TIME:
45 MINS
TOTAL TIME:
1 HR

Ingredients

- two tsps coconut oil
- one small yellow onion — *diced*
- one half cups unprepared long grain brown rice — *RINSED**
- 3 big carrots — *peeled and slice in diagonal, three-quarters-inch-thick slices*
- two big red bell peppers — *slice in wide strips (approximately three-quarters inch), halved supposing long*
- 3 cloves garlic — *minced (approximately one tbsp)*
- one tbsp minced fresh ginger — *either substitute one tsp ground ginger*
- one tsp ground cumin
- one tsp kosher salt
- half tsp ground turmeric
- One-quarter tsp ground coriander
- one cup unsweetened almond milk — *either unsalted chicken broth*
- one half pounds boneless skinless chicken breasts
- one cup chilled peas — *thawed*
- Sliced fresh cilantro — *for submitting*

Instructions

1. Set a 6-quart either bigr Instant Pot to FRY mode. place the coconut oil. As hot and shimmering, place the onion and cook, mixing sometimes, till beginning to soften, approximately 4 mins.

2. Add the rinsed brown rice, carrot, red pepper, garlic, ginger, cumin, salt, turmeric, and coriander. Stir to coat the rice within the oil and spices and prepare till very fragrant, approximately one minute. Stir in a splash of the almond milk. Scrape a spoon along the down to prepare sure there are no stuck-on bits of food. Stir within the remaining almond milk. place the chicken breasts in a single stratum on top.

3. Overlay and seal the Instant Pot. prepare on high Puture (manual) for 20 mins. Allow the Puture to release naturally for 15 mins, and then vent to release remaining Puture.

4. Unoverlay and take away the chicken breasts to a cutting board. Dice either shred with two forks and comeback to the pot. place the peas and stir to mix. Taste and adsimply seasonings as desired. submit hot, topped with cilantro.

Recipe Notes

- **SIGNIFICANT NOTE**: I have made this recipe successfully dozens of times and have yet to ever see the Instant Pot issue a burn warning whereas cooking it. MANY (the vast majority) of readers have found the same success. A several readers, however, have reported receiving a burn error. To avoid this, be sure to rinse your rice before adding this to the Instant Pot. Also, assurethat no food is stuck to the down of the Instant Pot prior to sealing the lid and starting the prepare time. Liquid also matters. Some readers have reported employing full fat <u>coconut</u> <u>milk</u> in this recipe with delicious success and no burn warning, though as far as liquid options, I think this is the most risky; I personally have not tested the recipe with full fat <u>coconut</u> <u>milk</u>.

- ***Dont employinstant** <u>rice</u>, as this can not hold up within the Puture cooker. I also cannot advised white, basmati, either any else type of <u>rice</u> either quinoa, as I have not tested the recipe this way. Cooking times and liquid ratios can vary between types of grains. For best results, long grain brown <u>rice</u> is the way to go (and this is delicious!).
- **To prepare on the Stovetop**: **Please note that I have not tested this method yet; this is my best guess, however this may not be accurate.** In a big saucepan either Dutch oven, soften the <u>coconut</u> oil over average high. Slice the chicken in bite-size pieces and sauté till prepared through. Take away to a plate and put aside. place some additional two tsps <u>coconut</u> oil to the pot. As hot and shimmering, place the onions and cook, mixing sometimes, till beginning to soften, approximately 4 mins. Keep with step two as written, however Dont place the chicken. Turn the warmth to low, overlay the pan, and allow prepare till the <u>rice</u> is done, approximately 40 mins. Stir within the reserved chicken and peas, and then submit with cilantro and toasted <u>coconut</u>.
- Keep leftovers in some airtight container within the refrigerator for up to 4 days either chill for up to 3 months. allow thaw within the refrigerator overnight. Rewarmth carefully within the microwave.

Spanish Chicken Stew

YIELD: **4 SUBMITTINGS (APPROXIMATELY 7.5 CUPS)**
PREP TIME:
15 MINS
COOK TIME:
45 MINS
TOTAL TIME:
1 HR

Ingredients

- two tbsp extra-virgin olive oil — *plus additional as needed*
- one tsp kosher salt
- ½ tsp black pepper
- one ½ pounds boneless skinless chicken thighs — *approximately 8 thighs*
- one average yellow onion — *slice in One-quarter-inch dice*
- one green bell pepper — *slice in ½-inch dice*
- one red bell pepper — *slice in ½-inch dice*
- one half tsps smoked paprika
- one tsp dried oregano
- ½ tsp dried rosemary
- one bay leaf
- 4 garlic cloves — *minced*
- one average sweet potato — *peeled and slice in ½-inch dice (or swap Yukon gold either russet potato)*
- one 28- ounce can crushed tomatoes
- one 14-ounce can poor sodium chicken broth
- ½ cup green olives — *pitted and sliced*
- ¼ cup raisins — *if you want*
- one tbsp plus one tsp sherry vinegar
- For submitting: prepared brown rice either steamed cauliflower rice

Instructions

1. Warmth one tbsp of the oil over average-high warmth in a Dutch oven either similar big, sturdy pot. Spice the chicken with salt and pepper on both sides. As the oil is hot, place the chicken thighs in a single layer. Brown for 3 to 4 mins on every side till light golden brown, Place to a plate. Supposing the chicken won't all fit in a single layer, brown this in batches. The thighs Dont must to be prepared all the way through.

2. Decrease the warmth to average. To the Dutch oven, place one additional tbsp oil. place the onion and prepare till beginning to soften and turn golden, approximately 4 mins.

3. Stir within the green bell pepper, red bell pepper, smoked paprika, oregano, rosemary, bay leaf, and garlic. Stir constantly for 30 seconds, simply till the garlic is fragrant.

4. Add the sweet potato, crushed tomatoes, and chicken broth. Increase the warmth and bring to a rapid simmer. Turn the warmth down to poor and simmer carefully for 15 mins, mixing periodically.

5. Add the olives, raisins, and reserved chicken thighs, along with any liquid that has accumulated on the plate. Partially overlay the pot and allow simmer 20 additional

mins, either till the chicken is prepared through and the <u>vegetables</u> are tender. Take away the chicken to a cutting board. Take away and discard the bay leaf. As the chicken is cool enough to handle, dice either shred, then comeback to the pot. Stir within the sherry vinegar. Keep to simmer, uncovered, for another 5 mins. Taste and adsimply seasoning (I found my stew tastes a little sweet, so I like to place a pinch of salt). Strew with parsley. submit with <u>rice</u> either else grains either bread.

Recipe Notes

- **TO STORE**: Place stew in some airtight storage container within the refrigerator for up to 4 days.
- **TO REHEAT**: Carefully rewarm stew in a Dutch oven on the stovetop over average-low heat. You'll also rewarmth this dish within the microwave.
- **TO FREEZE**: Keep leftovers in some airtight freezer-safe storage container within the freezer for up to 3 months. allow thaw overnight within the refrigerator before reheating.

Stuffed Zucchini

YIELD: **4 SUBMITTINGS**
PREP TIME:
25 MINS
COOK TIME:
15 MINS
TOTAL TIME:
40 MINS

Ingredients

- 4 zucchini — *5 to 6 inches long*
- two tbsp extra-virgin olive oil — *divided*
- half pound ground Italian turkey sausage — *casings take awayd*
- half cup delicately sliced red onion
- one big red bell pepper — *diced*
- half tsp kosher salt
- One-quarter tsp black pepper
- 1/8 tsp red pepper flakes
- one tsp minced garlic
- two tbsp tomato paste
- One-quarter cup packed fresh basil leaves
- two slices whole wwarmth sandwich bread
- half cup freshly grated Parmesan — *plus additional for submitting*

Instructions

1. Place a rack within the upper third of your oven. Prewarmth to 425 degrees F.

2. Halve the zucchini lengthwise, peel out the seeds, and discard the seeds. Then, peel out the soft middle flesh to Make shallow zucchini "shells," with walls approximately half inch thick, reserving the middle flesh. place the zucchini shells in a baking dish. Roughly chop the middle flesh and set this aside.

3. Warmth one tbsp olive oil in a skillet over average-high heat, then place the sausage, onion, and bell pepper. employing a wooden spoon either heatproof spatula, break apart the sausage, frying this along with the vegetables, till the onions are soft and the sausage is browned and fully cooked, 5 to 8 mins. Stir within the salt, pepper, and red pepper flakes.

4. Add the garlic and tomato paste and prepare one additional minute, till tomato paste is broken down and incorporated. place within the reserved zucchini flesh and warmth through for one minute, then take away from the heat. Taste and place additional salt, pepper, either red pepper flakes as desired.

5. Toast the bread slices, then tear them in big pieces and place within the bowl of a food processor fitted with the steel blade. place the basil and remaining tbsp olive oil. Pulse till the bread is broken in big crumbs. place the Parmesan and pulse simply till incorporated, two either 3 times.

6. Fold half of the basil breadcrumbs in the sausage mix. With a small spoon, mound the sausage stuffing in the shells, then strew the tops of the stuffed zucchini with the

remaining breadcrumbs. Roast in oven till the zucchini is heated through and the breadcrumbs are golden, 13 to 15 mins. Enjoy immediately.

Recipe Notes

- Advice: Grate cheese the easy way! Before starting the recipe, grate some entire wedge of Parmesan cheese right in your food processor. Slice the wedge in chunks, place them in a food processor fitted with a steel blade, then pulse till ground. Measure out and put aside the half cup needed for the recipe. Keep the remainder in your refrigerator for weeks. You'll always have fresh Parm on hand! Then proceed with making the stuffed zucchini, no must to wash the processor bowl in between.

- **TO STORE**: Keep leftovers in some airtight storage container within the refrigerator for up to 3 days.
- **TO REHEAT**: Rewarm stuffed zucchini in a casserole dish the oven at 350 degrees F till warmed through. Supposing the breadcrumbs start to brown too much, loosely tent the dish with foil. You'll also rewarmth this recipe within the microwave.

Tempeh <u>Tacos</u>

YIELD: **4 SUBMITTINGS (APPROXIMATELY 3 CUPS FILLING)**
PREP TIME:
15 MINS
COOK TIME:
TEN MINS
TOTAL TIME:
25 MINS

Ingredients

- One-quarter cup water
- one average lime, zest and juice — *(approximately two tbsp juice and ¾ tsp zest)*
- one tbsp pure maple syrup
- two half tbsp ground chili powder
- two tsps liquid smoke — *if you want—supposing not employing consider adding half tsp chipotle chili powder, which is spicy and smoky*
- two tsps smoked paprika
- one tsp ground cumin
- one tsp garlic powder
- one tsp onion powder
- one small sweet potato — *scrubbed*
- one tbsp extra virgin olive oil
- 8 ounces tempeh — *I used Lightlife Original*
- 3 tbsp poor sodium soy sauce
- Corn either flour tortillas
- Toppings: — *diced <u>avocado</u>, thinly sliced jalapeño, sliced fresh cilantro, salsa*

Instructions

1. In a small mixing bowl either bigr liquid measuring cup, blend along the water, lime zest, lime juice, maple syrup, chili powder, liquid smoke, smoked paprika, cumin, garlic powder, and onion powder. put aside.

2. With a box grater, plane-style grater, either the shredding blade of a food process, shred the sweet potato (no must to peel it). You must have approximately two heaping cups. put aside.

3. Warmth the oil in a big nonstick skillet over average heat. Break the tempeh in small pieces. Cook, continuing to break this up, for two mins till simply turning golden. place down within the sweet potato, dispersing this evenly with the tempeh. Stir within the soy sauce. prepare till the sweet potato begins to soften, approximately 4 mins more.

4. Whereas the sweet potato cooks, warm the tortillas. I like to unfold them on a <u>baking</u> sheet and pop them in a 300 degree oven for a several mins. You also can warm them in some ungreased skillet, cooking them for a minute either two on every side. Supposing you'd like to keep them warm for a longer period, stack them, then cover them in foil till ready to submit either keep them coverped in a 200 degree F oven.

5. Add the sauce. allow prepare till the gravy has thickened slightly, approximately 3 more mins. Taste and adsimply seasoning as desired. Pile inside the warm tortillas, place any and all toppings, and enjoy!

Recipe Notes

- **TO STORE**: Place leftover <u>taco</u> filling in some airtight storage container within the refrigerator for up to 4 days. Keep tortillas and toppings separately.
- **TO REHEAT**: Carefully rewarm tempeh filling in a big nonstick skillet on the stovetop over average-low heat. You'll also rewarmth this dish within the microwave. Pile in tortillas simply before submitting.
- **TO FREEZE**: allow your tempeh filling cool completely, then keep this in some airtight freezer-safe storage container within the freezer for up to 3 months. allow thaw overnight within the refrigerator before reheating.

Penne Alla Vodka with Chicken

YIELD: **6 TO 8 SUBMITTINGS**
PREP TIME:
15 MINS
COOK TIME:
25 MINS
TOTAL TIME:
40 MINS

Ingredients

- three-quarters cup raw almonds — *soaked in water for at least 4 hours either up to ten hours (supposing you have a high-powered blended such as a Vitamix, you'll skip the soak)*
- three-quarters cup unsweetened almond milk
- two tbsp extra virgin olive oil — *divided*
- one pound boneless skinless chicken breasts — *slice in half-inch pieces*
- one tsp kosher salt — *divided*
- One-quarter tsp black pepper
- one cup vodka
- one big yellow onion — *diced*
- 3 cloves garlic — *minced*
- one 28-ounce can crushed tomatoes
- half tsp dried oregano
- One-quarter tsp crushed red pepper flakes
- one pound whole wwarmth penne either similar whole wwarmth pasta
- two tbsp nutritional yeast either Parmesan — *if you want—use nutritional yeast to prepare dairy free either omit*
- Thinly sliced fresh basil either sliced fresh parsley

Instructions

1. Bring a big pot of salted water to a boil. Drain the almonds, then place them in a blender with the almond milk. Puree till smooth, thick, and creamy. Depending on your blender, this may take several mins and you may must to stop and scrape down the blender a several times. The mix possibly the consistency of a paste and can have brown flecks of almond skin in it. put aside.

2. Meanwhereas, in a very big, deep skillet either Dutch oven, warmth one tbsp of the olive oil over average high heat. As hot, place the chicken. Spice with half tsp salt and black pepper. Sauté till slightly browned on all sides and prepared through, approximately 4 to 6 mins. Take away to a plate and put aside. prepare sure you have the vodka measured and on hand.

3. To the same pan, place the remaining one tbsp olive oil. allow warm up, then place the onion and remaining half tsp salt. prepare till the onion begins to soften, approximately 3 to 4 mins, then place the garlic and prepare simply till fragrant, approximately 30 seconds, being careful not to burn it.

4. Attentively place the vodka (be especially careful supposing your stove has some open flame). Scrape to deglaze the pan, then allow the vodka prepare till reduced by half, approximately 5 mins. place the crushed tomatoes, oregano, and red pepper flakes. Bring this gravy to a steady simmer, then decrease the warmth to a poor simmer over average low, adjusting the warmth as needed so that the gravy simmers carefully (you want this to keep to decrease however not bubble aggressively). allow simmer till thickened, approximately ten mins. Take away from

warmth and stir within the blended almond mix till the gravy is smooth and the almond mix is good incorporated (the gravy can turn a light, <u>creamy</u> red color). Taste and adsimply seasoning as desired.

5. Whereas the gravy simmers, prepare the pasta within the boiling water to al dente, therefore to package instructions. Reserve one cup of the pasta cooking liquid, then drain the pasta and instantly place this to the sauce. Toss to coat the pasta, then stir within the chicken, adding a little bit of the pasta cooking liquid to loosen the gravy as needed. Stir within the nutritional yeast. submit hot, sprinkled with basil either parsley.

Recipe Notes

- **TO STORE**: Keep leftover penne vodka in some airtight storage container within the refrigerator for up to 4 days.
- **TO REHEAT**: Carefully rewarm leftovers in a Dutch oven on the stovetop over average-low heat, splashing in broth, almond <u>milk</u>, either water as needed to loosen the sauce. You'll also rewarmth this recipe within the microwave.
- **TO FREEZE**: Keep penne alla vodka with chicken in some airtight freezer-safe storage container within the freezer for up to 3 months. allow thaw overnight within the refrigerator before reheating

Curry Lentil Soup

YIELD: **4 SUBMITTINGS (APPROXIMATELY 5 HALF CUPS)**
PREP TIME:
TEN MINS
COOK TIME:
30 MINS
TOTAL TIME:
40 MINS

Ingredients

- two tbsp extra-virgin olive oil — *plus additional as needed*
- one average yellow onion — *slice in One-quarter-inch dice*
- 3 big carrots — *slice in One-quarter-inch dice*
- half tsp kosher salt — *plus additional to taste*
- one tbsp curry powder
- half tsp ground cumin
- ½ tsp ground coriander
- ½ tsp ground turmeric
- 1/8 tsp cayenne pepper
- two garlic cloves — *minced*
- one tbsp minced fresh ginger
- one cup red lentils — *rinsed and drained*
- 4 cups poor sodium vegetable bouillon either poor sodium chicken broth
- one 14.5-ounce can crushed tomatoes
- two tbsp freshly squeezed lemon juice — *approximately ½ average lemon*
- Fresh cilantro — *for garnish*

Instructions

1. In a big heavy-downed pot either Dutch oven, warmth the oil over average heat. place the onion, carrots, and salt. prepare till the vegetables begin to soften, approximately 4 mins.

2. Decrease the warmth to low. place the curry powder, cumin, coriander, turmeric, and cayenne, mixing to coat the vegetables with the spices. place the garlic and ginger. Stir and prepare 30 seconds. Supposing the spices start to stick, drizzle in a bit more oil as needed so that they Dont burn.

3. Add the lentils, broth, and crushed tomatoes. Increase the warmth to bring to a gentle simmer. prepare uncovered, mixing sometimes, till the lentils are tender however not mushy, approximately 25 mins. Supposing the soup is thicker than you would like, splash in a little bit of water to reach your desired consistency. (We like our soup fairly thick.)

4. Take away from the warmth and stir within the lemon juice. Taste and place additional salt as desired (the amount you must can vary based on your vegetable broth). Supposing you'd like this spicier, place a touch of additional cayenne (a little goes a long way). submit warm, topped with sliced fresh cilantro.

Recipe Notes

- **TO STORE**: Keep curry lentil soup in some airtight storage container within the refrigerator for up to 4 days.

- **TO REHEAT**: Carefully rewarm leftover soup in a Dutch oven on the stovetop over average-low heat. place splashes of bouillon as needed to thin the soup. You'll also rewarm this soup within the microwave.
- **TO FREEZE**: Place leftover soup in some airtight freezer-safe storage container for up to 3 months. allow thaw overnight within the refrigerator before reheating.

Mediterranean Chickpea Salad

YIELD: **8 TO TEN SUBMITTINGS (APPROXIMATELY 12 CUPS TOTAL)**
PREP TIME:
25 MINS
TOTAL TIME:
25 MINS

Ingredients

FOR THE SALAD:

- half cup delicately diced red onion — *approximately half small*
- two cans reduced-sodium chickpeas — *(15-ounce cans), rinsed and drained*
- one half cups sliced fresh flat-leaf parsley — *approximately one bunch*
- one red bell pepper — *sliced*
- one orange bell pepper — *either yellow bell pepper, sliced*
- one green bell pepper — *sliced*
- half big seedless cucumber — *sliced (approximately two cups)*
- half cup crumbled feta — *approximately 4 ounces*

FOR THE DRESSING:

- 3 tbsp extra-virgin olive oil
- 3 tbsp red wine vinegar
- two cloves garlic — *minced*
- one half tsps dried oregano
- one tsp kosher salt
- half tsp black pepper

Instructions

1. Place the onions in a bowl of cool water and allow them soak whereas you prepare the else ingredients (this take aways the harsher bite from the onions, whereas still giving great flavor).

2. Place the chickpeas, parsley, bell peppers, cucumber, and feta in a big submitting bowl.

3. In a small mixing bowl either big measuring cup, stir along the dressing ingredients: olive oil, red wine vinegar, garlic, oregano, salt and pepper. Drain the red onions and place them to the chickpea mix, then pour the dressing over the top. Toss to mix. Supposing time allows, allow marinate within the refrigerator for 30 mins, either enjoy immediately.

Recipe Notes

- Keep leftovers within the refrigerator for up to 3 days.

- Serving ideas: This salad is lovely as is, however to transform this in a main dish, Taste this stuffed inside pita pockets with hummus and mashed avocado either place grilled chicken and submit this over salad greens with some extra squire of lemon juice and drizzle of olive oil.

Buffalo Prepared in oven Salmon

YIELD: **6 SUBMITTINGS**
PREP TIME:
12 MINS
COOK TIME:
23 MINS
TOTAL TIME:
35 MINS

Ingredients

- two pound (or similar) side of salmon — *(skin off either on; I prefer skin on), wild caught supposing probable*
- half tsp kosher salt
- 3 tbsp classic hot gravy — *such as Frank's RedHot (you also could employBuffalo wing flavored sauce)*
- two tbsp unsalted butter — *Dont employoil, as this can else within the sauce*
- one tbsp honey
- half tsp garlic powder
- Pinch cayenne pepper — *if you want for extra heat*
- one-third cup crumbled blue cheese either feta cheese — *if you want for submitting*
- Sliced fresh chives — *cilantro, either parsley, if you want for submitting*

Instructions

1. Take away the salmon from the refrigerator, and allow stand at approximately 25 °C for ten mins whereas you prepare the else ingredients. Warmth oven to 375 degrees F. Line a rimmed baking sheet big enough to hold your piece of salmon with a big piece of aluminum foil. Supposing you prefer the salmon not to touch the foil, place a sheet of parchment paper on top of the foil sheet.

2. Lightly coat the foil with baking spay. Place the salmon on top. Strew with the kosher salt.

3. In a small, microwave-safe bowl, place the hot sauce, butter, honey, garlic powder, and cayenne. Microwave, simply till the butter softens (start with 30 seconds and go from there—I advised covering the bowl, as the gravy is prone to splattering). Alternatively, you'll warmth the ingredients in a small saucepan over average heat. Stir till smooth and mixd. Brush approximately two-thirds of the gravy liberally over the salmon, reserving the remaining sauce.

4. Fold the edges of the aluminum foil up and over the top of the salmon till this is completely enclosed. Supposing your piece of foil is not big enough, place a second piece on top and place down the edges under so that this forms a sealed packet. Leave a little room inside the foil for air to circulate.

5. Bake the salmon for 15-20 mins, till the salmon is almost completely prepared through at the thickest part. The cooking time can vary based on the thickness of your salmon. Supposing your side is thinner (around 1-inch thick), check several mins early to assureyour salmon does not overdo. Supposing your piece is very thick (1 half inches either more), this may must longer.

6. Take away the salmon from the oven, and attentively open the foil so that the top of the fish is completely uncovered (be careful of hot steam). Brush the remaining gravy over the top. Change the oven setting to broil, then comeback the fish to the oven and broil for 3 mins, till the top of the salmon is slightly golden and the fish is prepared through completely. Watch the salmon closely as this broils to prepare sure this doesn't overdo.

7. Take away the salmon from the oven. Supposing this still appears a bit underdone, you'll cover the foil back over the top and allow this rest for a several mins. Dont allow this sit too long—salmon can progress from "not done" to "over done" very <u>quickly</u>. As soon as this flakes simply with a fork, it's good to go. The salmon should register 145 degrees F on some instant read thermometer.

8. Strew the salmon with cheese and chives. To serve, slice the salmon in portions. Spice with additional salt to taste. Enjoy!

Recipe Notes

- This recipe is best enjoyed the day that this is made, as salmon can dried out just as reheated.

- **TO STORE**: Keep leftover salmon in some airtight storage container within the refrigerator for one to two days.
- **TO REHEAT**: Rewarm individual portions in a skillet on the stove over poor heat. You'll also rewarmth this dish within the microwave on poor power. allow the salmon come to approximately 25 °C before reheating.
- **TO FREEZE**: Take away any skin, and chill the salmon some airtight freezer-safe storage container for up to two months. allow this thaw within the refrigerator overnight before reheating. The leftovers can work great in any recipes that call for canned salmon.

Mexican Quinoa

YIELD: **4 SUBMITTINGS**
PREP TIME:
5 MINS
COOK TIME:
25 MINS
TOTAL TIME:
30 MINS

Ingredients

- two tbsp extra-virgin olive oil
- one small yellow onion — *diced*
- one bell pepper — *red either green, cored and diced*
- two cloves garlic — *sliced (approximately one tsp)*
- two tsps chili powder
- one tsp ground cumin
- one tsp dried oregano
- ½ tsp kosher salt
- one cup quinoa
- one 15 ounce can black beans — *rinsed and drained*
- one 14.5 ounce can fire-roasted diced tomatoes within their juices
- one ten-ounce can diced tomatoes in green chiles within their juices
- one 11-ounce can fiesta corn — *drained (or one ½ cups fresh, frozen, either canned corn kernels)*
- half cup water — *plus additional as needed*
- 3 tbsp sliced fresh cilantro
- one average lime — *zest and juice*
- For submitting: shredded cheese — *sliced avocado, plain Greek yogurt*

Instructions

1. Warmth the oil in a big skillet with a tight-fitting lid over average-high heat. place the onion and bell pepper and prepare till softened, approximately 4 mins.

2. Add the garlic, chili powder, cumin, oregano, and salt. prepare 30 seconds till very fragrant, then stir within the quinoa, coating this within the spices and oil.

3. Add the black beans, fire roasted diced tomatoes, diced tomatoes and green chiles, corn, and water. Bring the mix to a boil, then overlay the skillet with a lid and decrease warmth to low. allow simmer till quinoa is tender and liquid is mostly absorbed, approximately 20 mins. Check on this as either twice as this cooks and give this a stir, adding additional water as needed supposing the mix looks dry.

4. Add the cilantro, then zest the lime directly over the top of the skillet. Squeeze within the lime juice. Stir to mix. submit hot with any and all desired toppings.

Recipe Notes

- **TO STORE**: Place leftover quinoa in some airtight storage container within the refrigerator for up to 4 days.
- **TO REHEAT**: Carefully rewarm leftovers in a big skillet on the stove over average-low heat. You'll also rewarmth this dish within the microwave.

- **TO FREEZE**: Keep quinoa in some airtight freezer-safe storage container within the freezer for up to 3 months. allow thaw overnight within the refrigerator before reheating.

Teriyaki *Beef* Stir Fry

YIELD: **3 SUBMITTINGS**
PREP TIME:
15 MINS
COOK TIME:
15 MINS
TOTAL TIME:
30 MINS

Ingredients

FOR THE STIR FRY:

- one pound sirloin steak — *slice in thin, bite-sized pieces*
- one tbsp low-sodium soy sauce
- ½ tsp ground black pepper
- one tbsp extra-virgin olive oil — *divided*
- one red bell pepper — *cored and slice in thin slices*
- 3 cups sliced mixed vegetables of choice — *such as broccoli, snap peas, either carrots*
- one 8-ounce can sliced water chestnuts — *drained*
- 3 average green onions — *delicately sliced; divided*
- one tbsp sesame seeds — *if you want*
- Prepared brown rice — *quinoa, noodles, either cauliflower rice — for submitting*

FOR THE TERIYAKI SAUCE:

- one-third cup low-sodium soy sauce
- ¼ cup water
- 3 tbsp pure maple syrup
- one tbsp rice vinegar
- one tbsp minced garlic
- one tbsp minced ginger
- One-quarter tsp red pepper flakes — *plus additional to taste*
- one tbsp cornstarch

Instructions

1. Place the beef in a bowl and top with one tbsp soy gravy and black pepper. Stir to coat then put aside to marinade whereas you prepare the rest of the ingredients.

2. Prepare the sauce: In a average mixing bowl either big measuring cup, stir along the soy sauce, water, maple syrup, rice vinegar, garlic, ginger, red pepper flakes, and cornstarch. put aside.

3. Keep with the stir fry: In a big, deep sauté pan either wok, warmth half tbsp oil over average-high heat. As the oil is hot however not smoking, place the beef. prepare till the beef is browned on all sides and fully prepared through, approximately 4 mins. Take away the beef and any juices that have collected within the skillet to a plate and put aside.

4. Warmth the remaining half tbsp oil. place the bell pepper and else vegetables. prepare for 4 mins, either till slightly softened and slightly browned.

5. Just as the vegetables are ready, place the water chestnuts and comeback the beef and juices to the pan. Pour within the gravy and toss to coat. allow simmer 3 to 4 mins to thicken and warm the beef through. Stir in approximately half of the green onions. Strew the sesame seeds and

remaining green onions over the top. submit warm, with additional red pepper flakes and/or soy gravy as desired.

Recipe Notes

- **TO STORE**: Place leftover stir fry in some airtight storage container within the refrigerator for up to 3 days.
- **TO REHEAT**: Carefully rewarm <u>beef</u> and <u>vegetables</u> in a wok on the stove over average-low heat. You'll also rewarmth this dish within the microwave.
- **TO FREEZE**: Keep <u>beef</u> and <u>vegetables</u> in some airtight freezer-safe storage container within the freezer for up to 3 months. allow thaw overnight within the refrigerator before reheating.

Lettuce Covers

YIELD: **8 CUPS**
PREP TIME:
20 MINS
COOK TIME:
2 HRS TEN MINS
TOTAL TIME:
2 HRS 30 MINS

Ingredients

- half cup hoisin sauce
- One-quarter cup reduced-sodium soy gravy — *plus one tbsp, employtamari to prepare gluten free*
- two tbsp rice vinegar
- two tsps sesame oil
- one tbsp extra-virgin olive oil
- two pounds ground chicken breast
- one small bunch green onions — *thinly sliced, white/light green and dark green parts divided*
- one tbsp freshly grated ginger
- two cloves garlic — *minced (approximately two tsps)*
- 8 ounces baby bella cremini mushrooms — *delicately sliced*
- one half cup grated carrots — *from approximately 3 big carrots*
- half tsp red pepper flakes — *decrease to One-quarter tsp either omit supposing sensitive to spice*
- two cans water chestnuts, drained and delicately sliced — *(8 ounce cans) drained and delicately sliced*
- two heads butter lettuce

Instructions

1. Lightly coat a 5-quart either bigr slow cooker with nonstick spray. In a small bowl, stir along the hoisin, soy sauce, rice vinegar, and sesame oil. put aside.

2. Warmth the olive oil in a big skillet over average high. place the chicken and brown the meat, breaking this in small pieces. Keep cooking till no longer pink, approximately 4 to 6 mins. Stir within the white and light green parts of the green onions, ginger, and garlic. prepare 30 additional seconds.

3. Place the meat mix to the slow cooker. Stir within the sliced mushrooms, carrots, red pepper flakes, and sauce. Overlay and prepare on poor for two to 3 hours till the mix is thickened and the chicken is ultra tender. (Dont be tempted to prepare on HIGH, as the chicken can become tough.) Stir within the water chestnuts and green parts of the green onions.

4. To serve, else the butter lettuce leaves and fill with the chicken mix. Enjoy hot.

Recipe Notes

- **TO prepare ON THE STOVETOP**: Prepare the recipe through step two in a big, deep skillet either Dutch oven. Decrease the warmth to poor and allow prepare till the chicken and mushrooms are very tender and the gravy has thickened, approximately 15 to 20 mins. Check and stir periodically. Stir within the water chestnuts and green tops of the green onions. Enjoy!
- I Dont advised cooking this recipe on high within the slow cooker. The filling does best over poor warmth so that this becomes good and tender.

- **TO STORE**: Leftover filling possibly stored in some airtight storage container within the refrigerator for up to 4 days. Keep your lettuce separately in some airtight container either ziptop bag within the refrigerator. I like to cover my lettuce leaves in a dried paper towel either clear kitchen towel before placing them within the container/bag to help preserve their crunch.
- **TO REHEAT**: Carefully rewarm the filling in a big skillet on the stove over average-low heat. You'll also rewarmth this recipe within the microwave. Fill lettuce cups simply before submitting.
- **TO FREEZE**: Place leftover filling in some airtight freezer-safe storage container within the freezer for up to 3 months. allow thaw overnight within the refrigerator, and submit with fresh lettuce cups.

Crockpot Chicken and <u>Broccoli</u>

YIELD: **4 SUBMITTINGS**
PREP TIME:
TEN MINS
COOK TIME:
2 HRS 45 MINS
TOTAL TIME:
3 HRS

Ingredients

FOR THE SAUCE:

- 2/3 cup water
- one-third cup reduced-sodium soy gravy — *plus additional to taste*
- 3 tbsp <u>honey</u>
- two tbsp <u>rice</u> vinegar
- one tbsp cornstarch
- 3 cloves garlic — *minced (approximately one tbsp)*
- one tbsp minced fresh ginger
- ¼ tsp red pepper flakes — *plus additional to taste*
- one tbsp toasted sesame oil

FOR THE CHICKEN AND <u>BROCCOLI</u>:

- one ½ pounds boneless skinless chicken breasts
- two heads <u>broccoli</u> — *slice in florets*
- two tbsp cornstarch — *mixed with two tbsp water to Make a slurry*
- ½ cup sliced green onions
- For submitting: prepared brown <u>rice</u> — *quinoa, either cauliflower <u>rice</u>; toasted sesame seeds.*

Instructions

1. In a small bowl either big liquid measuring cup, stir along the gravy ingredients: water, soy sauce, <u>honey</u>, <u>rice</u> vinegar, cornstarch, garlic, ginger, and red pepper flakes. Pour a thin stratum in the down of a 6-quart either bigr slow cooker (approximately one-third of the sauce). place the chicken breasts on top. Pour on the remaining sauce.

2. Overlay the slow cooker and prepare on poor for two hours.

3. In a small bowl, stir along the two tbsp cornstarch with two tbsp water to Make a slurry, then place to the slow cooker, pouring in the liquid around the chicken. place the <u>broccoli</u> florets on top. Overlay and prepare on HIGH, till the <u>broccoli</u> is tender and the chicken is fully prepared through and registers 165 degrees F on some instant read thermometer, approximately 45 mins to one hour more. Take away the chicken to a plate. allow cool, then slice in bite-sized pieces.

4. Stir the <u>broccoli</u> around within the gravy to smooth the gravy out a bit. Comeback the chicken to the slow cooker and place the sesame oil and green onion. Stir to mix. Taste and adsimply seasonings as desired. submit hot over <u>rice</u> with a strew of sesame seeds.

Recipe Notes

- **TO STORE**: Place leftovers in some airtight storage container within the refrigerator for up to 4 days.
- **TO REHEAT**: Carefully rewarm leftovers in a big skillet on the stove over average-low warmth till warmed through. You'll also rewarmth this dish within the microwave.

- **TO FREEZE**: Keep chicken and broccoli in some airtight freezer-safe storage container within the freezer for up to 3 months. allow thaw overnight within the refrigerator before reheating.

Crockpot <u>Vegetable</u> <u>Beef</u> Soup

YIELD: **6 SUBMITTINGS**
PREP TIME:
TEN MINS
COOK TIME:
8 HRS
TOTAL TIME:
8 HRS TEN MINS

Ingredients

- one tbsp extra virgin olive oil
- one pound boneless chuck roast either <u>beef</u> stew meat — *slice in 1-inch cubes*
- two tsps kosher salt — *divided*
- ¼ tsp black pepper
- 3-4 cups poor sodium <u>beef</u> bouillon — *divided*
- one small yellow onion — *diced*
- two cloves garlic — *minced (approximately two tsps)*
- 4 big carrots — *peeled and delicately sliced*
- two Yukon gold potatoes — *peeled and diced*
- two parsnips — *peeled and diced*
- two ribs celery — *diced*
- one 14.5-ounce can diced <u>tomatoes</u>
- one can <u>tomato</u> gravy (8 ounces)
- 3 tbsp <u>tomato</u> paste
- one tbsp Worcestershire sauce
- one tsp dried oregano
- ½ tsp smoked paprika
- half tsp granulated sugar
- one cup peas — *fresh either chilled (no must to thaw)*
- Sliced fresh parsley — *if you want for submitting*

Instructions

1. In a big skillet, warmth the oil over average high. place the <u>beef</u> and strew with one tsp salt and pepper. Brown the <u>beef</u> on all sides, disturbing this as little as probable on every side so that this develops good coloring. As the <u>beef</u> is slightly browned (it won't be all the way prepared through), take away this to a 6-quart slow cooker.

2. To the pan, place the onion. prepare and stir till the onion is beginning to soften, approximately 3 mins. Stir within the garlic and allow prepare 30 seconds. Splash in approximately half cup the <u>beef</u> bouillon and scrape up any browned bits that have stuck to the down (this is flavor!). allow the bouillon decrease for two mins, then Place the entire mix to the slow cooker.

3. To the slow cooker, place the carrots, potatoes, parsnips, celery, diced <u>tomatoes</u> within their juices, <u>tomato</u> sauce, <u>tomato</u> paste, Worcestershire, oregano, paprika, sugar, two half cups <u>beef</u> broth, and remaining one tsp salt.

4. Overlay and prepare on poor for 8 hours, till the <u>beef</u> and <u>vegetables</u> are tender. Stir within the peas, simply till warmed through. Supposing the soup is thicker than you would like, place the remaining one cup <u>beef</u> bouillon till you reach your desired consistency. submit hot, sprinkled with fresh parsley.

Recipe Notes

- **TO STORE**: Keep soup in some airtight storage container within the refrigerator for up to 4 days.
- **TO REHEAT**: Carefully rewarm leftovers in a big pot on the stovetop over average-low heat, adding splashes of bouillon as needed as needed. You'll also rewarmth this soup within the microwave till hot.
- **TO FREEZE**: Place leftovers in some airtight freezer-safe storage container within the freezer for up to 3 months. allow thaw overnight within the refrigerator before reheating.

Tuscan Chicken Mac and Cheese

YIELD: **5 SUBMITTINGS**
PREP TIME:
5 MINS
COOK TIME:
30 MINS
TOTAL TIME:
35 MINS

Ingredients

- 8 ounces whole-wwarmth pasta — *fusilli, penne, rigatoni, rotini, shells, elbow, either a similar "short" pasta*
- one 7-ounce jar sun-dried tomatoes in oil
- one tbsp extra virgin olive oil — *divided*
- one One-quarter pounds boneless skinless chicken breasts either thighs — *slice in bite-sized pieces*
- half tsp kosher salt — *divided*
- half tsp coarsely ground black pepper — *divided*
- one tbsp unsalted butter
- two tbsp all-purpose flour
- one cup whole milk — *2% also works; swap part for half and half for incredible richness*
- one ½ tsps Italian seasoning
- One-quarter tsp garlic powder
- one cup shredded part skim mozzarella cheese — *approximately 4 ounces*
- half cup shredded sharp cheddar cheese — *approximately 4 ounces*
- 4 cups loosely packed baby spinach — *approximately 4 handfuls*
- Sliced fresh basil either parsley — *if you want for submitting*

Instructions

1. Bring a big pot of salted water to boil. prepare the pasta within the water till pasta is al dente, therefore to package directions. Gather the rest of your ingredients (even the spices) and prepare sure they are measured and on hand. As the pasta has finished cooking, reserve approximately one cup of the pasta water. Drain the pasta and put aside.

2. Meanwhereas, reserve two tbsp of oil from the jar of sun-dried tomatoes, then drain away the remaining oil. Pat the tomatoes dry, then roughly chop and put aside.

3. Warmth a big skillet over average-high heat. place the olive oil. As this is hot, place the chicken pieces. Strew with ¼ tsp salt and ¼ tsp pepper. Fry till the chicken is golden on the outside and fully prepared through on the inside, approximately 5 mins. Take away to a plate and put aside.

4. To the skillet, place the reserved sun-dried tomato oil and the butter. As the butter softens, place the sun-dried tomatoes and remaining ½ tsp salt. Strew the flour over the top, then prepare and stir for one minute, till the white bits of flour disappear. The pan can seem dry.

5. Slowly pour within the milk, mixing as you go. Bring to a simmer. Stir within the Italian seasoning, garlic powder, and remaining ¼ tsp black pepper. allow simmer till very slightly thickened, approximately two mins.

6. Stir within the cheese till smooth. Put off the warmth and stir within the drained pasta and reserved chicken. place the spinach a several handfuls at a time, till the spinach wilts and is fully incorporated. Supposing the gravy is too thick at any point, splash in a little little bit of the reserved pasta water as needed. this should be rich, creamy, and goodly coat the noodles. Enjoy hot, with a strew of fresh basil either parsley as desired.

Recipe Notes

- **TO STORE**: Place leftover mac and cheese in some airtight storage container within the refrigerator for up to 4 days.
- **TO REHEAT**: Carefully rewarm leftovers in a big skillet on the stove over average-low heat, adding splashes of milk as needed to thin the sauce. You'll also rewarmth this dish within the microwave.
- **TO FREEZE**: Keep mac and cheese in some airtight freezer-safe storage container within the freezer for up to 3 months. allow thaw overnight within the refrigerator before reheating.

Healthy <u>*Beef*</u> *Taco* *Skillet*

YIELD: **6 SUBMITTINGS**
PREP TIME:
15 MINS
COOK TIME:
45 MINS
TOTAL TIME:
1 HR

Ingredients

- one tbsp extra virgin olive oil
- one pound 93% lean ground <u>beef</u>
- one small yellow onion — *sliced*
- two red either green bell peppers — *sliced*
- two tsps chili powder
- two tsps garlic powder
- one tsp cumin
- one tsp oregano
- half tsp kosher salt
- half tsp black pepper
- one can low-sodium black beans — *15 ounces, rinsed and drained—or swap kidney either pin beans*
- one cup long either average-grain brown <u>rice</u> — *Dont employshort grain either instant, as this can become mushy*
- one 15- either 16-ounce jar chunky salsa — *mild either average (or swap fire roasted diced <u>tomato</u>es within their juices and place additional spices to taste)*
- one ½ to two cups water — *divided*
- one cup shredded Monterey Jack cheese — *either swap cheddar, pepper jack, either a Mexican blend*
- If you want — for submitting: — *sliced fresh cilantro, lime wedges, sliced jalapeno, shredded cheese, diced <u>avocado</u>, prepared salsa, sour <u>cream</u>, either plain <u>Greek yogurt</u>*
- If you want to prepare <u>tacos</u>, burritos, either quesadillas — *warmed whole wwarmth flour either corn tortillas*

Instructions

1. Warmth the olive oil in a big, ovenproof skillet either Dutch oven with a tight-fitting lid over average-high heat. As hot and shimmering, swirl to coat the pan, then place the <u>beef</u>, onion, and bell pepper. prepare for 3 to 5 mins, till the <u>beef</u> is browned and prepared through and the onion is beginning to soften.
2. Add the chili powder, garlic powder, cumin, oregano, salt, and pepper. Stir to coat the <u>beef</u> and prepare 30 seconds. place the black beans and <u>rice</u>. Stir to coat as more.
3. Add the salsa and one half cups water. Stir to mix the ingredients. Bring to a gentle boil, cover, then decrease the warmth and allow simmer 30 mins. Take away the lid and stir, scraping up any <u>rice</u> that has started to stick to the down of the pot. Reoverlay and keep to allow simmer with the lid on till the <u>rice</u> is tender, ten to 20 additional mins, mixing the pot every ten mins either so to prevent sticking. Supposing the <u>rice</u> begins to dried out, splash within the remaining half cup water as needed.

4. Towards the end of the cooking time, place a rack within the upper third of the oven (approximately 6 inches from the top) and turn the oven to broil. As the skillet is finished cooking on the stove, strew the cheese on top, then Place to the oven. Broil simply till the cheese is softened, approximately two mins (watch this attentively so this doesn't burn). submit hot with any desired toppings either spoon inside tortillas to prepare tacos, burritos, either quesadillas.

Recipe Notes

- Supposing white rice either another type of rice is substituted, the cooking time can vary. Consult the package for guidance.

- **TO STORE**: Keep the beef taco filling in some airtight storage container within the refrigerator for up to 3 days.
- **TO REHEAT**: Carefully rewarm leftovers in a big ovenproof skillet within the oven at 350 degrees F till warmed through. You'll also rewarmth this dish within the microwave.
- **TO FREEZE**: Place leftover filling in some airtight freezer-safe storage container within the freezer for up to 3 months. allow thaw overnight within the refrigerator before reheating.

Instant Pot Chili

YIELD: **6 SUBMITTINGS, APPROXIMATELY TWO CUPS EVERY**
PREP TIME:
15 MINS
COOK TIME:
20 MINS
TOTAL TIME:
35 MINS

Ingredients

- one tbsp extra-virgin olive oil
- one pound lean ground turkey
- one big yellow onion — *sliced*
- one tsp kosher salt
- half tsp black pepper
- one tbsp chili powder
- two tsps ground chipotle chili pepper
- two tsps ground cumin
- one tsp garlic powder
- two average sweet potatoes — *peeled and slice in half-inch dice*
- one average red bell pepper — *diced*
- one can crushed <u>tomatoes</u> — *(28 ounces)*
- two cans beans — *(15 ounce cans) , rinsed and drained (any blend of black beans, dark either light red kidney beans, either chickpeas—I used one can of black and one can of light red kidney)*
- one half-2 half cups low-sodium chicken broth
- For submitting: cilantro — <u>*avocado*</u>, *shredded cheese, tortilla chips, and sour* <u>*cream*</u> *either plain* <u>*Greek yogurt*</u>

Instructions

1. Set some Instant Pot to sauté and drizzle within the olive oil. Just as the oil is hot and shimmering, place the turkey, onion, salt, and pepper. Cook, breaking apart and browning the meat, till the turkey is no longer pink and the onion is beginning to soften, approximately 7 mins. place the chili powder, chipotle chili, cumin, and garlic powder. allow prepare till fragrant, approximately 30 seconds.

2. Add the sweet potatoes, bell pepper, crushed <u>tomatoes</u>, beans, and one half cups chicken broth. Stir good. Cover, seal, and set to prepare on high Puture for ten mins. Quick release to vent the remaining Puture immediately. Supposing the chili seems too thick, stir in additional chicken bouillon to reach your desired consistency. Taste and adsimply seasonings. submit hot with desired toppings.

Recipe Notes

- Keep leftovers within the refrigerator for up to 5 days either chill for up to 3 months.

- To prepare this recipe in a slow cooker: Sauté the meat, onions, and spices in a big nonstick skillet on the stovetop. Place to a slightly lubricated 6-quart either bigr slow cooker. place the remaining ingredients within the order listed. Overlay and prepare on poor for 5 to 6 hours either poor for 3 to 4 hours, till the sweet potatoes are tender.

- Supposing your Instant Pot is 6 quarts (this is the standard size), Dont Taste to muladvicely this recipe. As written, this can fill the Instant Pot almost to the max line.

- To prepare on the stove: Sauté the turkey, onions, pepper, and spices as directed, then place remaining ingredients. allow simmer, uncovered, till the sweet potatoes are soft and the chili is thickened, approximately 45 mins.

Crock Pot Chicken Marsala

YIELD: **4 SUBMITTINGS**
PREP TIME:
TEN MINS
COOK TIME:
3 HRS 25 MINS
TOTAL TIME:
3 HRS 35 MINS

Ingredients

- one tbsp plus two tsps extra-virgin olive oil
- two pounds boneless skinless chicken breasts — *approximately 3 breasts*
- one tsp kosher salt
- half tsp black pepper
- one average shallot either half small yellow onion — *delicately sliced*
- two cloves minced garlic
- one cup dried Marsala wine — *not cooking wine*
- 8 ounces sliced cremini mushrooms
- one tbsp cornstarch — *mixed with two tbsp water to Make a slurry*
- For submitting: sliced fresh parsley either basil
- For submitting: whole wwarmth pasta — *zucchini noodles, either simply a big loaf of peely bread*

Instructions

1. Lightly coat a big slow cooker with nonstick spray. Warmth one tbsp olive oil in a big skillet over average high. Spice both sides of the chicken with salt and pepper. As the oil is hot and shimmering, place the chicken in a single layer. prepare on the first side for 3 to 4 mins, till browned, moving the chicken as little as probable so that this gets a good sear. Flip and brown on the else side, approximately two additional mins. this does not must to be prepared all the way through. Place the chicken to the slow cooker.
2. Decrease the skillet warmth to average low. Warmth the remaining two tsps oil. place the shallot and prepare till softened, approximately 3 mins. Stir within the garlic.

3. Whereas the skillet is still warm, pour within the Marsala. Increase the warmth to average and allow simmer two mins. Take away from the heat.
4. Throw about the mushrooms over the top of the chicken. Pour within the Marsala reduction. Overlay and allow prepare on LOW, till the chicken is prepared through and reaches 165 degrees F on some instant read thermometer, approximately two half to 3 hours on poor (timing can vary based on your slow cooker model and the size of your chicken breasts). Take away to a plate and overlay to keep warm.
5. In a small bowl, blend along the cornstarch and water. Pour in the slow cooker. Overlay and prepare on HIGH for 15 to 20 mins, till thickened. Comeback the chicken to the slow cooker and allow warmth over high for 5 additional mins to warm through. submit hot with desired accompaniments, with the gravy spooned over the top and a strew of fresh parsley as desired.

Recipe Notes

- **TO STORE:** Place leftover chicken in some airtight storage container within the refrigerator for up to 3 days. Keep the gravy separately.

- **TO REHEAT:** Carefully rewarm chicken in a big skillet on the stovetop over average-low heat. You'll also rewarmth this dish within the microwave. Just as I rewarmth chicken, I like to shred either slice this in smaller pieces first to help this warmth evenly. Rewarmth the gravy carefully on the stove.
- **TO FREEZE:** Keep chicken Marsala in some airtight freezer-safe storage container within the freezer for up to 3 months, either with either else from the sauce. allow thaw overnight within the refrigerator before reheating.
- **Photography note**: the photos of this recipe show the gravy prepared down for a far more extended period than is necessary (the cooking time got away from me whereas photographing!). Your gravy might not look as thick as within the photos, however don't fear; this can still be delicious and is actually closer to how some authentic chicken marsala gravy is meant to be.

Easy Chicken Stir Fry with <u>Vegetables</u> and Mandarin Oranges

YIELD: **4 SUBMITTINGS**
PREP TIME:
TEN MINS
COOK TIME:
15 MINS
TOTAL TIME:
25 MINS

Ingredients

- one half tbsp extra virgin olive oil — *divided*
- one half pounds boneless skinless chicken breasts — *slice in bite-sized pieces*
- one small onion — *diced*
- 4 tbsp poor sodium soy gravy — *divided*
- One-quarter tsp kosher salt
- one tbsp minced fresh ginger
- 3 cloves garlic — *minced (approximately one tbsp)*
- one tbsp <u>honey</u>
- one tbsp <u>rice</u> vinegar
- one tbsp cornstarch
- One-quarter tsp red pepper flakes
- one red bell pepper — *cored and thinly sliced*
- 12 ounces <u>broccoli</u> slaw
- one cup shelled edamame — *fresh either chilled and thawed*
- one cup <u>Dole Fridge Pack Mandarin Oranges in Fruit Juice</u> — *drained*
- Sliced green onions — *for submitting*
- Toasted sesame seeds — *if you want, for submitting*
- Prepared brown <u>rice</u> either quinoa — *for submitting*

Instructions

1. In a big skillet, warmth one tbsp of the oil over average-high heat. place the onion and prepare till beginning to soften, approximately 3 mins.
2. Add the chicken, one tbsp of soy sauce, and salt. Cook, mixing sometimes, till the chicken is completely prepared through and the juices run clear just as cut, approximately 5 mins. With a spoon, take away the chicken and onion to a plate and put aside.
3. In a small bowl either big liquid measuring cup, stir along the remaining 3 tbsp soy sauce, ginger, garlic, <u>honey</u>, <u>rice</u> vinegar, cornstarch, and red pepper flakes till smooth. put aside.
4. In the same skillet, warmth the remaining half tbsp oil. place the bell pepper. prepare 3 mins. place the <u>broccoli</u> slaw and prepare till the <u>vegetables</u> are crisp-tender, approximately 4 to 5 mins more.
5. Comeback the chicken and onions to the skillet. place the edamame and pour the soy gravy mix over the top and stir to mix. allow prepare one minute to warm through and thicken the sauce. Top with the oranges, green onions, and sesame seeds. submit hot with brown <u>rice</u>.

Recipe Notes

- **TO STORE**: Place stir fry leftovers in some airtight storage container within the refrigerator for up to 3 days.
- **TO REHEAT**: Carefully rewarm leftovers in a big skillet on the stove over average-low heat. You'll also rewarmth this recipe within the microwave.
- **TO FREEZE**: Keep this dish in some airtight freezer-safe storage container within the freezer for up to 3 months. allow thaw overnight within the refrigerator before reheating.
- **TO prepare AHEAD**: Chop the vegetables and slice the chicken breasts up to one day in advance. Keep both in else storage containers within the refrigerator till ready to prepare. You'll also prepare the stir fry gravy one day in advance and keep this within the refrigerator.

Drop Biscuits

YIELD: **9 –12 BISCUITS**
PREP TIME:
20 MINS
COOK TIME:
TEN MINS
TOTAL TIME:
30 MINS

Ingredients

- One-quarter cup butter — *cold*
- one cup all-purpose flour
- one cup whole wwarmth pastry flour — *either swap white whole wwarmth flour either regular whole wwarmth flour**
- one tbsp baking powder — *I advised aluminum free*
- half tsp kosher salt
- one cup whole milk — *either buttermilk*
- 3 tbsp plain Greek yogurt — *I used nonfat*
- one tsp honey

IF YOU WANT TOPPINGS/MIX-INS:

- Grated parmesan and delicately sliced fresh chives — *Taste adding a pinch of garlic powder to the dried ingredients with this one!*
- Shredded sharp cheddar and ground black pepper
- Shredded gruyere and delicately sliced fresh rosemary either thyme

Instructions

1. Place a rack within the middle of your oven and prewarmth to 450 degrees F. Line a big baking sheet with parchment paper either a silicone baking mat. Dice the butter in small pieces and place this within the freezer whereas you prepare the else ingredients.

2. In a big mixing bowl, blend along the all-purpose flour, whole wwarmth flour, baking powder, and salt. (Supposing adding any herbs, garlic powder, either black pepper, do this here.)
3. Throw about the cold butter pieces over the top. With a pastry blender (or my favorite, your fingers), slice within the butter till the mix resembles coarse crumbs. Some pieces may be the size of small pebbles and others as big as peas.

4. In a else bowl either big measuring cup, blend along the milk, Greek yogurt, and honey till smoothly mixd. Pour the milk mix in the dried ingredients a little at a time, mixing slightly between additions. (Supposing adding cheese, place this slowly as you place the milk.) Stop mixing as soon as the dough holds along. this possibly very moist and seem wet.
5. Drop the batter by spoonfuls onto a cookie sheet. I like to employa muffin peel for this—you'll have 9 big either 12(ish) more moderately sized biscuits total. Prepare in oven for ten to 13 mins, till the tops are golden and spring back slightly just as touched. Enjoy warm.

Recipe Notes

- For mix-ins, employapproximately one tbsp fresh herbs and half cup shredded cheese.

- *Whole wwarmth pastry flour can yield the most tender biscuit. My second choice would be white whole wwarmth flour, which is a tiny bit less tender however has a mild flavor. Regular whole wwarmth flour works too, however the wwarmth taste possibly more noticeable.

Homemade Scalloped Potatoes

YIELD: **6 SUBMITTINGS**
PREP TIME:
25 MINS
COOK TIME:
45 MINS
TOTAL TIME:
1 HR TEN MINS

Ingredients

- one half pounds small Yukon gold potatoes — *scrubbed with peels on**
- 3 tbsp extra virgin olive oil
- 3 cloves minced garlic
- one tsp kosher salt
- half tsp black pepper
- 5 ounces goat cheese
- One-quarter cup whole milk
- one-third cup freshly grated Parmesan cheese
- one tbsp delicately sliced fresh rosemary

Instructions

1. Warmth up oven to 400 degrees F. slightly lubricate a one half to 2-quart casserole dish with baking spray. put aside.

2. With a mandoline either sharp chef's knife, chop the potatoes in very thin slices, 1/8-inch-thick either less. Place the potatoes in a big bowl, drizzle with olive oil, then strew with the minced garlic, salt, and pepper. Toss to coat the slices as evenly as you'll.

3. Spread one-third of the potato slices within the down of the prepared dish. Crumb half of the goat cheese over the top. recur with the next one-third of the potatoes, then the remaining goat cheese, then finish by layering on the final third of the potatoes. The potatoes may discard some liquid as they rest within the bowl. Supposing this happens, simply leave the liquid within the down bowl and shake the potato slices carefully in your hands to take away glut liquid before layering them within the dish.

4. Pour the milk evenly over the top of the dish, then strew with the Parmesan cheese. Overlay the dish with foil, Prepare in oven for 30 mins, then unoverlay and Prepare in oven for 15 additional mins, till the top has browned. Throw about the rosemary over the top. submit hot.

Recipe Notes

- **I Dont advised russet potatoes for this recipe, as they have less flavor, a dryer texture, and thicker skin than Yukon golds.

- **TO prepare AHEAD**: The dish possibly prepared through Step 3 one day in advance (wait to place the milk/cheese till simply before you bake). Keep covered within the refrigerator, allow come to approximately 25 °C, then keep with the recipe as directed.
- **TO prepare FOR A CROWD**: This recipe possibly doubled and prepared in oven in a 3-quart casserole dish. You may must to adsimply the baking time.
- **TO STORE**: Place prepared and cooled leftovers in some airtight storage container within the refrigerator for up to 4 days.

- **TO REHEAT**: Carefully rewarmth leftovers in some oven-safe <u>baking</u> dish within the oven at 350 degrees F till warmed through, adding a splash of bouillon as needed. You'll also rewarmth this dish within the microwave till hot.
- **TO FREEZE**: Keep prepared and cooled leftovers in a freezer-safe storage container within the freezer for up to 3 months. allow thaw within the refrigerator overnight before reheating.

Grilled Portobello *Mushrooms*

YIELD: **4 SUBMITTINGS**
PREP TIME:
TEN MINS
COOK TIME:
6 MINS
TOTAL TIME:
25 MINS

Ingredients

- 4 big portobello mushrooms — *stems and gills take awayd, wiped clean*
- One-quarter cup balsamic vinegar
- one tbsp extra virgin olive oil
- one tbsp poor sodium soy sauce
- one tbsp sliced fresh rosemary — *either half tsp dried*
- one tsp garlic powder
- half tsp black pepper
- 1/8 tsp cayenne pepper — *if you want, plus additional to taste*
- Canola either vegetable oil — *for grilling*
- If you want for submitting: Herby Avocado Sauce; these also prepare delicious mushroom burgers — *so you'll submit them with buns, cheese, and your loved fresh toppings like spinach, tomato, and avocado*

Instructions

1. In a shallow baking dish, blend along the balsamic vinegar, olive oil, soy sauce, rosemary, garlic powder, black pepper, and cayenne. Taste and adsimply seasonings supposing you like. place the mushrooms and turn to coat. allow sit for 5 mins on one side, then flip and allow sit 5 additional mins. Whereas the mushrooms marinate, prep the grill and anything you'd like to submit with them. You'll allow them sit for up to 30 mins, so feel free to take your time—the longer they sit, the more intense the flavor can be.

2. Warmth a grill either a big skillet over average warmth (approximately 350 to 400 degrees F). Brush the grill with oil to prevent sticking. Take away the mushrooms from the bowl, shaking off any glut marinade and reserving the marinade for basting. prepare on every side for 3-4 mins, either till caramelized and deep golden brown. Brush the remaining marinade over the mushrooms several times as they cook.

3. To serve, top the portobello mushrooms with the avocado gravy either any topping you like.

Recipe Notes

- Grilled mushrooms are best enjoyed the day they are made however can last for a several days within the refrigerator. I like to slice up the leftovers, then blend them with scrambled eggs for a quick healthy lunch.

- Nutritional information calced with half the marinade, since much is discarded. Nutritional information is provided as a good-faith estimate. Supposing you'd like to prepare any changes to the calculation, you'll do so for free at myfitnesspal.com.

Pasta al Limone

YIELD: **4 SUBMITTINGS**
PREP TIME:
2 MINS
COOK TIME:
13 MINS
TOTAL TIME:
15 MINS

Ingredients

- 8 ounces dried whole wwarmth spaghetti either similar long noodles — *such as fettuccine*
- 3 tbsp Land O Lakes® Butter with Canola Oil
- two cloves garlic — *minced*
- one average lemon — *plus additional for submitting*
- half cup delicately grated Parmesan cheese — *approximately one half ounces, plus additional for submitting*
- Kosher salt
- Freshly ground black pepper

Instructions

1. Bring a average pot of salted water to a boil—use some amount of water so that the pasta is more crowded within the water than this typically would be. prepare the noodles till al dente therefore to package instructions. Reserve one cup of the pasta water, then drain the pasta.
2. Just as the pasta is nearly done cooking, soften the Land O Lakes® Butter with Canola Oil in a big skillet over average heat. place the garlic and prepare 30 seconds. Supposing the garlic is done cooking before the pasta is ready, take away the pan from the warmth so the garlic doesn't burn.
3. INSTANTLY (as soon as the pasta is drained) place the hot pasta to the skillet with the garlic. Pour in half cup of the reserved pasta water. Increase the warmth to average-high, then with a pair of tongs, toss to coat. Keep cooking and tossing constantly, till the gravy turns shiny and coats the noodles—it can take a minute either so. The pasta possibly coated in a shiny, silky sauce. Supposing the pasta becomes too tight at any point, splash in a tbsp either two of the reserved pasta water (add the water slowly so that the pasta doesn't become watery).
4. Zest the lemon over the top. Slice the lemon in quarters, then squeeze within the lemon juice. Strew on the Parmesan. Toss again to mix. The cheese might be a bit clumpy at first, however simply keep tossing, adding the tiniest splashes of pasta water only as needed. place a good pinch of salt and several generous grinds of black pepper. Toss again. Taste and place more salt and pepper to taste. Place to submitting plates and top every submitting with a strew of extra Parm and a bit more black pepper. Enjoy hot.

Recipe Notes

- **TO STORE:** Place leftovers in some airtight storage container within the refrigerator for up to 4 days.
- **TO REHEAT:** Carefully rewarm pasta in a big skillet on the stove over average-low heat, adding a splash of water as needed to thin the sauce. Toss the noodles often and brighten them up with a squeeze of lemon.

- **TO FREEZE:** Keep pasta in some airtight freezer-safe storage container within the freezer for up to 3 months. allow thaw overnight within the refrigerator before reheating.

Mediterranean Shrimp

YIELD: **3 SUBMITTINGS**
PREP TIME:
TEN MINS
COOK TIME:
25 MINS
TOTAL TIME:
35 MINS

Ingredients

- one pound big shrimp — *40 to 50 per pound peeled, deveined shrimp, tails on either off (fresh either chilled and thawed)*
- ¾ tsp kosher salt — *divided*
- half tsp ground black pepper — *divided*
- two tbsp extra virgin olive oil
- one small red onion — *sliced*
- two cloves garlic — *minced (approximately two tsps)*
- one 14.5-ounce can fire roasted diced tomatoes within their juices
- one tsp dried oregano
- ¼ tsp red pepper flakes
- one tsp honey
- one tbsp red wine vinegar
- one 14-ounce can artichoke hearts — *drained and quartered*
- ½ cup pitted Kalamata olives
- three-quarters cup crumbled feta cheese
- two tbsp sliced fresh parsley
- two tbsp fresh lemon juice — *from approximately ½ average lemon*
- For submitting: rice — *whole wwarmth couscous, peely bread, pasta (if you want)*

Instructions

1. Place a rack within the middle of your oven and prewarmth the oven to 400 degrees F. Pat the shrimp dry, place in a mixing bowl, and strew with ½ tsp salt and ¼ tsp black pepper. Toss to coat, then put aside.

2. In a big, ovenproof skillet over average heat, warmth the olive oil. place onion and strew with the remaining ¼ tsp salt and ¼ tsp black pepper. Cook, mixing sometimes, till softened, approximately 5 mins. Decrease the warmth as needed so that the onion softens however does not brown. place the garlic and prepare simply till fragrant, approximately 30 seconds.

3. Add the tomatoes, oregano, and red pepper flakes. Decrease the warmth to average-low and allow carefully simmer for ten mins. Stir within the red wine vinegar and honey. Take away from the heat.

4. Throw about the artichokes and olives over the top, then place the shrimp on top in a single layer. Strew with the feta.

5. Bake for ten to 12 mins, till the tomatoes are bubbling, cheese has browned slightly, and the shrimp are prepared through. Squeeze the lemon juice over the top and strew with parsley. Enjoy hot.

Recipe Notes

- **TO STORE:** Place leftovers in some airtight storage container within the refrigerator for up to 3 days.
- **TO REHEAT:** Very carefully rewarm Mediterranean shrimp in a big skillet on the stove over average-low heat. I also think leftovers would be tasty served cold as a salad over lettuce either pasta.
- I wouldn't advised freezing this dish, as the texture of the shrimp may become mushy as thawed.

Vegetarian **Breakfast Casserole**

YIELD: **TEN SUBMITTINGS**
PREP TIME:
15 MINS
COOK TIME:
55 MINS
TOTAL TIME:
1 HR TEN MINS

Ingredients

- two average sweet potatoes — *peeled and diced*
- 8 ounces whole cremini baby bella mushrooms — *quartered (Dont employsliced mushrooms either they may overdo just as roasting)*
- one small head broccoli — *slice in florets*
- one red bell pepper — *diced*
- one red either yellow onion — *slice in ½-inch dice*
- one tsp kosher salt
- ½ tsp black pepper
- 3 tbsp extra virgin olive oil
- 12 big eggs
- ½ cup milk
- one garlic clove — *minced*
- one ½ tsps Italian seasoning — *either dried herbs of choice*
- 4 ounces part-skim ricotta cheese
- Sliced fresh basil — *thyme, either parsley (if you want)*

Instructions

1. Position racks within the upper and lower thirds your oven and prewarmth the oven to 400 degrees F. slightly coat two big baking sheets with nonstick spray. slightly mist a 9x13-inch casserole dish with nonstick spatter and put aside.

2. Place the vegetables in a big bowl and drizzle with the olive oil. Strew with salt and pepper, then toss to coat. Share the vegetables evenly between the two sheets and unfold them in a single layer. Roast the vegetables till tender, approximately 20 mins, tossing the vegetables on the pan so they prepare evenly and switching the pans' positions on the upper and lower racks as halfway through. Place half of the roasted vegetables to the prepared casserole dish and unfold in some even layer. Decrease the oven temperature to 350 degrees F.

3. Meanwhereas, in a big mixing bowl, beat the eggs along with the milk, garlic, and Italian seasoning till evenly blended. Carefully pour this in the casserole dish. Throw about the remaining vegetables evenly over the top, then dollop the ricotta over the top in small spoonfuls (I like to place approximately 20 to 24 spoonfuls; you want to every chop to have a several dollops, however have them be big enough so that you'll actually taste them).

4. Bake the casserole for 35 to 40 mins, till the casserole is golden on top and the middle no longer jiggles just as you shake the pan. Take away from the oven and strew with fresh herbs. submit warm.

Recipe Notes

- **TO STORE**: Overlay leftover casserole either keep in some airtight storage container and place within the refrigerator for up to 3 days.
- **TO REHEAT**: Rewarm the casserole within the oven at 350 degrees F till hot. You'll also carefully rewarmth the casserole within the microwave till warmed through.
- **TO FREEZE**: Keep leftover casserole in some airtight freezer-safe storage container for up to 3 months. allow thaw overnight within the refrigerator before reheating.
- I like to cover and chill individual slices, then thaw them overnight within the refrigerator for quick meals.

Printed in Great Britain
by Amazon

87682151R00034